Little Ones

Lori Cameron

LitPrime Solutions
21250 Hawthorne Blvd
Suite 500, Torrance, CA 90503
www.litprime.com
Phone: 1 (209) 788-3500

© 2021 Lori Cameron. All rights reserved.

No part of this book may be reproduced, stored in a retrieval system, or transmitted by any means without the written permission of the author.

Published by LitPrime Solutions   01/28/2021

ISBN: 978-1-953397-78-2(sc)
ISBN: 978-1-953397-79-9(hc)
ISBN: 978-1-953397-75-1(e)

Library of Congress Control Number: 2021900719

Any people depicted in stock imagery provided by iStock are models, and such images are being used for illustrative purposes only.

Certain stock imagery © iStock.

Because of the dynamic nature of the Internet, any web addresses or links contained in this book may have changed since publication and may no longer be valid. The views expressed in this work are solely those of the author and do not necessarily reflect the views of the publisher, and the publisher hereby disclaims any responsibility for them.

Little Ones

SONG IN Bb

Little One, Little one Jesus loves you
Little one, little one. Know He Cares
Little one, little one, I am here for you
Little one, little one, don't you worry
Little one, little one, He is here for you
Little one, little one, Jesus cares for you

Blusie? Asked the trembling dog, "Who is Jesus?"

We all have at some stage in our life felt rejection and loneliness. This is never pleasant to go through. We are left hurting and longing for someone to come along and say that they care for us and truly mean it, and that everything will be alright.

Dear reader, are you lonely and wanting to have someone truly care for you? In my life I have suffered rejection many times over the years, nevertheless, there is someone who suffered severe rejection by those He loved, and His name is Jesus.

Jesus came into this world wanting to mend and heal broken hearts and heal those with terrible diseases. His love is never ending, and He is reaching out to you today saying... "Come unto me all you who are heavily burdened, and I will give you rest.

In this book, I have portrayed my beautiful dogs, each one of these beautiful creatures have been rejected and hurt. This book is showing these dogs reaching out for one another and sharing the love of Jesus Christ to a hurting world.

Be inspired to reach out for Jesus, because, He is reaching out for you.

All Scripture from the KJV

Hello, Hello!! Anika, look over there, said Blusie, there is a dog crying.

Blusie trotted over to the distressed dog

Hello, "whatever is wrong, Oh, please don't cry." Look at all those tears. "Oh dear, oh dear, come, come, little one, let me help you."

Just then, Anika came up to see what was going on. "Hello Blusie, Oh dear, what's going on?" said Anika. "I'm trying to find out" said Blusie, "but the little one keeps crying.

"Come, Blusie, let us go and comfort him," said Anika.
So, Blusie and Anika wandered over to the upset dog who couldn't stop crying.

Blusie came near to the upset dog and gently put her paw on the little one's head and Anika sat beside the little dog

"Now," said Blusie, "What is with all these tears?" and gently licked his tears away. "Please, little one, tell us what this is all about."

The young dog, in between great sobs, said, "no one wants me, I keep getting rejected by people, and all I want is to be loved."

Psalm 9:9-10

9. The Lord also will be a refuge for the oppressed, a refuge in times of trouble. 10. And they that know thy name will put their trust in thee: for thou, Lord, hast not forsaken them that seek thee.

As they walked along, Anika said, "My owners only wanted me for breeding, I was so dirty, they never ever cleaned me, it was horrible, and I was out in all weathers. They don't care that we like to be dry and warm, they were only interested in what they could make out of me with my puppies."

"Then one day, this lady came and saw me and rescued me. She told my owners that she was going to take me to her home and that she was going to report them for abuse and mishandling of dogs.

"Well, I was so happy, I couldn't believe this was happening to me. The lady gently lifted me onto the back seat of her car and took me to her home.

ANIKA

"When I arrived at this lady's home, it was wonderful, and guess what? She took me into this room and helped me into this place with a curtain around it and washed me with this nice smelling soap, then dried me and brushed me. Oh. I felt so good, so light and clean, I have never felt anything like this before. Then she told me that I am her little baby girl and that she is going to call me Anika and that she loves me and will always keep me safe because she is now my mum."

Philippians 4:4, 7

4. Rejoice in the Lord always: and again, I say rejoice. 7. And the peace of God, which passes all understanding, shall keep your hearts and minds through Christ Jesus.

BLUSIE

Then Blusie said, "I use to live on this farm where I was kept in this awful place. All they wanted me for was breeding. I was so worn out and dirty. My babies were always taken away from me.

These kind people came and rescued me and now I live with Anika's mum and she is always telling me that she loves me and that I was her little baby girl too."

When the little dog heard this from Blusie he started to cry even more. "I w i s h... Oh, boo! hoo! oh, how I wish I could live with you too. Boo! hoo! I am so unhappy; I wish I could be loved"

Then Blusie started to sing a song to the little dog.

In Bb for Piano

| Little One | Little One | Jesus loves you |
| C Bb D | C Bb D | F G A C |

| Little One | Little One | Know He cares |
| C Bb D | C Bb D | F A G F |

| Little One | Little One | I am here for you |
| C Bb D | C Bb D | F G A Bb C |

| Little One Little One | | Don't you worry |
| C Bb D C Bb D | | F A G F |

| Little One | Little One | He is here for you |
| C Bb D | C Bb D | F G A Bb C |

| Little One | Little One | Jesus cares for you |
| C Bb D | C Bb D | F A G F F |

Blusie, said the little dog, who is Jesus?

Blusie looked upon the little dog and smiled. Little one, said Blusie, Jesus has His arms out waiting for you to say to Him, I am here Jesus, please come into my life? I need you

Isaiah 26:3-4

Thou wilt keep him in perfect peace, whose mind is stayed on thee: because he trusted in thee.

Trust ye in the Lord for ever: for in the Lord Jehovah is everlasting strength.

John 14:27

Peace I leave with you, my peace I give unto you: not as the world giveth, give I unto you. Let not your heart be troubled, neither let it be afraid.

As they wondered along, an idea came to Blusie and Anika. They looked at each other and knew what the other was thinking.

"What if the little dog came to live with us."

Let's go and see mum. There she is over there by the pond. As they wondered over towards her, the lady turned around and saw them coming.

"Well hello", said mum, "What are you girls up to"?

Blusie who has always been a talker, started to make noises and turning her body around, and nodding with her head for her mum to follow. "What's the matter Blusie"? said mum. Again, Blusie got mouthy "Awooh,

Awooh," showing mum that she wanted her to follow

As they walked along Blusie and Anika ran up to the little dog who was still crying. Mum ran up and said, "Well hello, who do we have here?"

"O dear, you poor little thing." Looking at the little dog, mum said, "You look so sad and frightened, what has happened to you?" Bending down to the dog, mum put her arms around the dog to comfort him. "What has happened to you?" The little dog continued to shake and cry in her arms. "Now, now, little one do not be afraid, you are safe with us.

"Come on girls," said mum to Blusie and Anika, "lets find him something to eat and drink." They took the little dog back to the house and fed him and gave him water. Oh, he was so thirsty, "Slurp, Slurp, Slurp, as he drank the water and hungrily, he ate the food all up, the food was gone in no time at all.

Then mum looked at the little dog and said, "How would you like a wash to make you feel better and be all nice and clean?" With that mum said, "Come on girls, let us go and give this little one a nice wash."

Stroking the dog, mum said, "Don't be afraid, we will look after you. "You are not on your own anymore, you can stay with us."

Mum brought the little dog in for a wash, "Oh how good this feels," the little dog thought to himself. After a wash and a good brush, the dog really started to feel better and gave a happy lick to the lady, who said, "would you like me to be your new mum too?" How about we call you Bailey, you are a lovely looking dog." With that Bailey wagged his tail and gave his new mum a great big kiss.

Then they all went out into the garden where Bailey found a ball and ran around and round in the garden with the ball in his mouth. "Oh, this is so wonderful, I am so happy," then he thought to himself about the song Blusie had sung to him and remembered Jesus and how He loved him too. "I am loved, and I am wanted." Bailey thought to himself. Hooray, and ran around and round in the garden again. "I am Loved, I am loved, never to be rejected again." Bailey sang to himself.

Romans 8: 35, 37-39

Who shall separate us from the love of Christ? Shall tribulation, or distress, or persecution, or famine, or nakedness, or peril, or sword?

Nay, in all these things we are more than conquerors through Him that loved us.

For I am persuaded, that neither death, nor life, nor angels, nor principalities, nor powers, nor things present, nor things to come.

Nor height, nor depth, nor any other creature, shall be able to separate us from the love of God, which is in Christ Jesus our Lord.

Bailey and Blusie ready for bed

Isaiah 41:10

Fear thou not; for I am with thee be not dismayed; for I am thy God: I will strengthen thee; yea, I will help thee; yea, I will uphold thee with the right hand of my righteousness.

Bailey and Blusie relaxing

EPILOGUE

Unfortunately, Anika passed away after a long illness at the ripe old age of 16 ½ years.

Anika was a precious little girl, who was very faithful and loving and who I loved very much.

Since 1997 I have rescued many Siberian Huskies. These beautiful creatures are such faithful companions and give back as much love as I give them, if not more.

Bailey is a lovely Retriever who has become a very faithful companion and follows me wherever I go.

Blusie is now 5years old and Bailey is 8 years old.

A HAPPY FAMILY

Lori Cameron lives in the hills of Wales in the UK with her precious dogs, now Blusie and Bailey.

Her inspiration comes from the love of her Lord Jesus Christ who is Lori's chief companion. Her love of the Lord and the love He has bestowed on her throughout the years is her strength and has become stronger with every passing moment as He continues to lead her on a wonderful journey with Him.

www.ingramcontent.com/pod-product-compliance
Lightning Source LLC
Chambersburg PA
CBHW021433070526
44577CB00001B/184